Macht

Fun-to-Solve

MAP MYSTERIES

by Lisa Trumbauer

NEW YORK • TORONTO • LONDON • AUCKLAND • SYDNEY
MEXICO CITY • NEW DELHI • HONG KONG • BUENOS AIRES

SCHOLASTIC
Teaching
Resources

For my parents, Fred and Sigrid Trutkoff,
who gave me my love for maps and travel.

Cover and interior design by Sydney Wright

Cover and interior illustration by Rebecca Thornburgh

ISBN 0-439-29704-4

Copyright © 2003 by Lisa Trumbauer

All rights reserved. Published by Scholastic Inc.

Printed in the U.S.A.

1 2 3 4 5 6 7 8 9 10   40   12 11 10 09 08 07 06 05 04 03

Contents

To the Teacher

At first glance, maps might seem a mystery to young learners. To the untrained eye, a map can look like nothing more than a jumble of lines, with no pattern or purpose. Even harder to decipher is the concept that a map is an illustration of a place from above. Unless you are actually flying above a place, how can you know what it looks like? Why, by looking at a map, of course!

Understanding how to use a map is just as important as understanding *why* people use maps. The mysteries in this book introduce children to simple maps drawn by the kids of Keen-I Detective Services (K.I.D.S.). Students will also work with maps they might have seen without realizing they were maps, such as mall maps, stadium maps, and library maps. Children will realize that maps show people how to get from place to place, as well as show physical aspects of an area, even those people can't readily see. The mysteries also introduce basic map components, such as color variation, symbols, map keys, the compass rose, and a grid. Students will come to learn that maps are not just for people who travel, but can be used to gain information and learn about places.

How to Use This Book

The mysteries in this book help children develop and practice key map skills. Read in order, the mysteries start with the basic understanding of a map as an illustration of a place from above. Then the maps invite students to build upon their knowledge by applying several map-reading skills in combination. Each mystery is about three pages long, followed by K.I.D.S. Clues—a simple explanation of a map concept that will point children in the right direction as they try to solve the mystery. A corresponding activity sheet accompanies each mystery. The sheet includes a map, plus instructions on how to use it to solve the mystery.

Before you begin working with the mysteries, reproduce copies of page 7 for each child. As a class, talk about the kids in K.I.D.S.—Keen-I Detective Services. Once children are familiar with the characters (Vanessa, Jasper, and Mari), select a map mystery to solve. You may choose to present a map mystery in several ways.

- Reproduce copies of the mystery and map for each child, challenging children to read and solve the mystery on their own.

- Reproduce copies of the mystery and map for small groups, encouraging students to work together to solve the mystery.

- Read the mystery aloud to the class and introduce unfamiliar map concepts and vocabulary. Pass out copies of the map page to individual children or small groups, and invite the class to solve the mystery together.

- Or, read the mystery aloud, then pass out copies of the map, as well as the mystery, for students to refer to as they solve the mystery on their own or in small groups.

The main idea children should get from these mini map mysteries is that maps are not something they should fear or view as complicated. Maps are simply another way to view the world around them. They are an ideal resource for gaining new information about their world, as well as a new perspective of what their world looks like.

Have fun being super sleuths as you solve these map mysteries!

Meet the Kids of K.I.D.S.:

Keen-I Detective Services

Vanessa: Vanessa loves a good adventure and helping others. What better way to do so than by starting her own detective agency? Along with her friends Jasper and Mari, Vanessa does her best to solve the mysteries that crop up in the neighborhood. It is her goal to help her friends and neighbors—and to have a fun time while doing it.

Jasper: Jasper likes to know the facts. He writes down everything people say and do, hoping someday he might be a writer. He likes being a part of K.I.D.S. because he thinks the detective adventures would make great action comic books, which he would like to write someday. He is a keen observer and one of Vanessa's best friends.

Mari: Mari is Vanessa's other best friend. She has a soft spot for animals, and she can often be found with her head buried in a book about animal characters. Mari thinks being a detective is fun, and she especially likes when they can help find missing animals or lost pets.

You! As you read each mystery, you'll be asked to help K.I.D.S. solve the case. Follow the directions to find out how!

The Hiding Hamster

Maps are special drawings people can use to locate places. There are many different kinds of maps. Some maps are pictures of places as seen from above.

Vanessa went to open the door of the clubhouse. Someone was knocking! Someone was seeking the services of K.I.D.S.

"He's gone!" the girl on the other side of the clubhouse door cried.

"Carmen! What's wrong?" Vanessa asked as she looked at the troubled girl.

"I just told you! He's gone!" Carmen wailed again.

"Who's gone?" Vanessa asked patiently.

"My pet hamster, Harry!"

Vanessa opened the door wider, and the girl came inside. Jasper and Mari, also detectives with the agency, took out pencils and paper to jot down all the facts. Vanessa, Jasper, Mari, and Carmen sat around the small table in the clubhouse.

"What happened?" Jasper asked importantly, his pencil already on his notepad.

"I was cleaning my room," Carmen explained. "Harry's cage is usually next to the window, on my bedside table. I moved the cage so I could move the bedside table and sweep underneath."

"Poor Harry!" Mari said. "Where did you move the cage?"

"I put it on my desk."

"What did you do next?" Vanessa asked.

"I swept, then I moved the table back. But when I went to get Harry and his cage, the cage was there, but Harry was gone!"

Jasper was busy scribbling notes. Vanessa was tapping her forehead. Mari scrunched her nose to ask another question. "Harry must be very scared. Did you search your room?"

"Of course I did!" Carmen wailed. "But I couldn't find Harry anywhere!"

"Hmm," Vanessa said thoughtfully. "Very puzzling."

"Can you help?" Carmen pleaded.

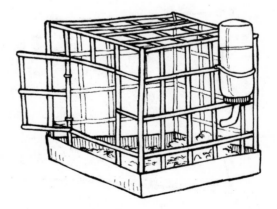

"Let's go to your house and see your room," Vanessa said.

Gathering their notes, the detectives of K.I.D.S. followed Carmen home. Upon entering her bedroom, they looked around without touching a thing.

Carmen took a piece of paper off her desk and handed it to Vanessa. "I don't know if this will help, but for a school project, we had to draw a map of our rooms. The maps had to include labels for furniture and special objects. As I looked for Harry, I checked off the places on the map that I searched."

Vanessa studied Carmen's map. Then she borrowed Jasper's notebook and drew a map of her own, labeling each object just as Carmen did. Vanessa compared her map to Carmen's.

"I think I know where Harry is!" Vanessa proclaimed.

Where is Harry hiding?

K.I.D.S. Clues

A map is a drawing of what a place looks like from above or below. You can use a map to see where things in a place are located. A floor plan is a kind of map. Floor plans can show where things such as furniture are located in a room or building.

Name _____

Carmen's Room

Here is the map Carmen made of her room:

Here is the map that Vanessa made:

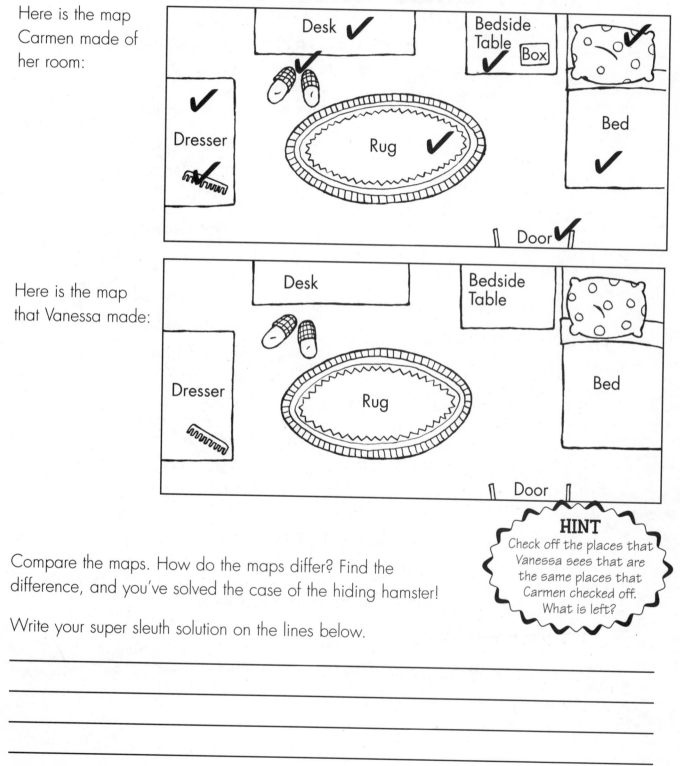

Compare the maps. How do the maps differ? Find the difference, and you've solved the case of the hiding hamster!

Write your super sleuth solution on the lines below.

HINT
Check off the places that Vanessa sees that are the same places that Carmen checked off. What is left?

_____
_____
_____
_____
_____

Mrs. Readsalot's Brooch

Maps have labels that tell the names of places. The labels provide information that the map doesn't have room to show.

Vanessa, Jasper, and Mari were at the library. They had a huge report to write on the pyramids of Egypt. The topic was cool. After all, how can you argue with learning about mummies?

But, being at the library wasn't as fun as solving mysteries, though.

"I wish we had another mystery to solve," Vanessa sighed as she thumbed through a large encyclopedia.

Jasper was taking notes. "Did you know that the organs in the dead body are removed before it's made into a mummy?"

"Did you know that they made cats into mummies, too?" Mari asked, holding up a book for them to see.

Vanessa sighed again. Ancient Egypt was just fine. But where was the mystery?

A scream from Mrs. Readsalot, the librarian, was the mystery she was looking for.

"My brooch! My brooch! It's gone!" Mrs. Readsalot shouted. For a librarian, she wasn't being very quiet.

"Sounds like a mystery that needs solving!" Vanessa said, jumping up from the table. Jasper and Mari followed.

"What seems to be the problem, Mrs. Readsalot?" Vanessa asked.

"I've lost my brooch!" she screeched again.

"What's a brooch?" Jasper whispered to Mari.

"I think it's, like, a fancy pin," she guessed.

"My brooch is a very old, very valuable pin," Mrs. Readsalot added. "It was a gift from my grandmother."

"What does it look like?" Jasper asked.

"It's quite large and shaped like a butterfly."

Jasper wrote down the details.

"Where did you go today?" Vanessa continued the questioning.

"I don't see how you kids can help," Mrs. Readsalot said glumly.

"We're not just kids. We're K.I.D.S.—Keen-I Detective Services," Vanessa assured her. "We've solved lots of mysteries.

We can help you get your brooch back."

Mrs. Readsalot still didn't look too sure. But she told them anyway. "Well, first I was in the media room. Then I crossed the library and went to the reference section. After rearranging the periodicals there, I went back to the media room, then to the children's section. From there, I had to go to the storage room to get some new books. I went back to the children's section, and then I looked up some books in the computer room. From there, let's see, I went across to the adult fiction shelves to put some returns away. And that's where we are now."

"Did you check each of these areas?" Vanessa asked smartly.

"Of course, dear," Mrs. Readsalot said. "It's gone, I just know it!"

"Maybe not," Vanessa said with confidence. Going back to the table, she took out a piece of paper and drew the rooms of the library. "Jasper, read off to me exactly where Mrs. Readsalot went." As he did, Vanessa drew lines to mark Mrs. Readsalot's path.

When she was finished, Vanessa sat back with victory in her eyes. "I think I know where Mrs. Readsalot's brooch is!"

Where did Mrs. Readsalot lose her brooch?

K.I.D.S. Clues

Maps have labels that tell the names of places. Some labels tell the names of rooms. This way, instead of a room just looking like a square or a rectangle, you can look at a map and identify the kind of room shown.

Name _____

Mrs. Readsalot's Library

Here is what Mrs. Readsalot told K.I.D.S. about her day at the library:

"Well, first I was in the media room. Then I crossed the library and went to the reference section. After rearranging the periodicals there, I went back to the media room, then to the children's section. From there, I had to go to the storage room to get some new books. I went back to the children's section, and then I looked up some books in the computer room. From there, let's see, I went across to the adult fiction shelves to put some returns away. And that's where we are now."

Here is a map of the library. With a red marker or crayon, draw a line from one room to the next to show where Mrs. Readsalot went.

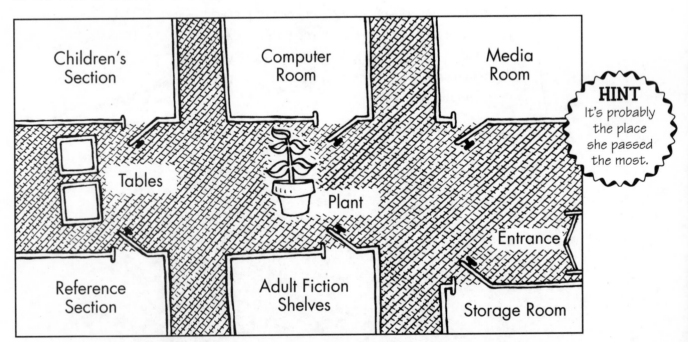

HINT
It's probably the place she passed the most.

Where might Mrs. Readsalot's butterfly brooch be? Circle the place on the map!

The Silly Surf Dude

Colors and symbols make it easier to identify different places on a map. Map keys, or legends, name what those colors and symbols stand for.

"Surf's up, dudes!" Jasper hollered as he rode his boogie board out in the ocean.

Mari turned to Vanessa. "And who does Jasper think he is?"

"King of the Waves, I guess," Vanessa said, rubbing on some sunscreen.

Mari adjusted her baseball cap on her head and put on her sunglasses. "Well, I'd rather be Queen of the Rays, if you get my meaning."

"Totally!" Vanessa said, lounging back on her beach towel.

Just then, Jasper ran up, flinging drops of water all over them.

"Jasper!" Mari exclaimed. "Watch what you're doing! You're getting us all wet!"

"Oh, sorry," Jasper said. "But did you see me catch that wave?"

"Sorry," Vanessa said. "We must have missed it. Now, could you move? You're blocking my sun."

"What? Oh, sure," Jasper said. "But first, you have to meet my new friend, Chip."

Mari lifted her glasses. The guy standing before her was a little older than Jasper, with dark hair that had streaks of white in it. He wore a seashell on a string around his neck. "New friend?"

"Yeah! And Vanessa, Chip here has a mystery for you to solve!"

This got Vanessa's attention. She sat up. "Mystery? What type of mystery?"

"Of the stolen-object kind."

"Just the kind I like!" Vanessa said, getting to her feet. "Tell me what happened."

As Chip told them his story, they walked across the beach to the snack bar.

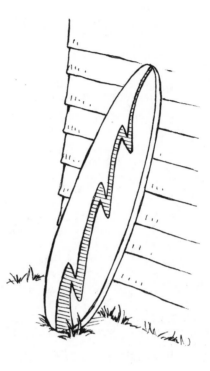

"Well, dudes, like I told your friend here, I got to the beach by walking on the path that goes through the dunes. I came out at the snack bar, where I leaned my surfboard against the wall. I went in to get something to eat, and when I came out, my surfboard was missing. Gone. Stolen. History."

"Pretty cool, huh?" Jasper said.

"Maybe," Vanessa said, thinking as she walked. "Let's get a juice and go over the details again."

While they waited in the snack bar line, Vanessa's eyes fell on a map of the beach area.

"Hey, Chip," she called out.

"Hey," he answered back lazily.

"Did you stop anywhere before you got to the snack bar?"

"Nah, just stopped here to get a soda."

"Did you pass any other buildings?"

He scratched his head. "I don't think so. Why?"

"I think you did," Vanessa said, getting out of line. "And I think I know where your surfboard is."

What happened to Chip's surfboard?

K.I.D.S. Clues

Some maps use colors to make it easier to tell one place from another. Maps also use symbols. Each symbol is a picture or pattern that represents a special place on the map. The symbols save space because they are smaller than the actual words or phrases needed to describe the places. The symbols and what they represent can be found in the map key.

Key	
🚻	Rest Rooms
🥤	Snack Bar

Name _____

By the Beach

Look at the map below. It shows the beach where Vanessa, Jasper, and Mari were spending the day. If you color in areas of the map, it will make other details easier to see. Follow these instructions to color the map.

1. Color the Salty Ocean blue.   **3.** Color the Dandy Dunes green.

2. Color the Sandy Beach yellow.

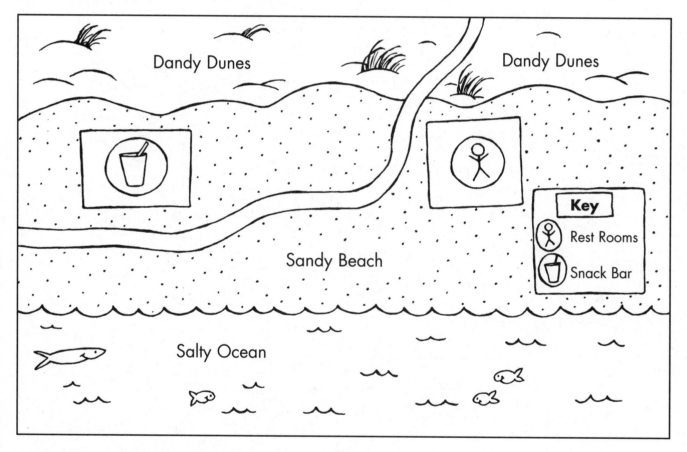

Now follow the path through the dunes to the beach. Use a pencil to show the path. What is the symbol for the building where the path comes out of the dunes? Draw it here:

What does this symbol mean? _____

Is this the same place that Chip says he went to first? _____

Where, then, might Chip's surfboard be? Write your ideas on the back of this page.

The Lost Lifeguard

Maps use symbols that can represent specific places.

It was a perfect summer day. The detectives of K.I.D.S. were taking a much-needed day off from solving mysteries. Vanessa, Jasper, and Mari were lounging at the neighborhood pool, waiting for the rest period to end. Seated on a bench beside the pool, they waited for the lifeguard to blow the whistle. That would mean all the kids could go back in the water.

They waited and waited.

"I think the fifteen-minute break is over, don't you?" Jasper asked impatiently.

"It is," Vanessa agreed. "Let's go to the pool office and see what's up."

When they got to the office, a group of kids was there ahead of them.

"I don't know what to tell you, kids," Mr. Schwimmer, the pool manager, said. "We can't find Leo. He's supposed to be the lifeguard on duty after the rest period. Until we find him, no one is allowed in the pool."

After a chorus of *aaaawwws* from the rest of the kids, Vanessa asked where Leo might have gone.

"I have no idea," Mr. Schwimmer shrugged. "He did leave this note, telling us where he'd be, but I don't understand the message."

"May I see it?" Vanessa asked.

Mr. Schwimmer shrugged again. "Sure. But I don't think you'll have any more luck than I did."

"Have no fear," Mari began.

"We're K.I.D.S.!" Jasper finished.

"I know you're kids, but—"

"K-I-D-S. As in Keen-I Detective Services," Vanessa said slowly.

Mr. Schwimmer looked at her blankly.

Vanessa shook her head and took the note. Jasper and Mari read the note over her shoulder.

"It's just a bunch of half sentences with pictures," Jasper noted.

"But the pictures look familiar," Mari pointed out.

"Yes, they do," Vanessa said slowly. "Hmm."

"I think it's some kind of surfer language," Mr. Schwimmer suggested. "Leo always has his mind on the beach, not this pool."

"It's not surfer language," Vanessa said. "But I think I do know what it is. Come on, guys!"

With Mari and Jasper following, Vanessa led them to the pool entrance. A huge map of the pool area hung beside the sign-in desk. Vanessa looked at the map. Then she looked at Leo's note.

Mr. Schwimmer came puffing up beside her. "So, if it's not surfer language, then what is it?"

"It's a language all its own," Vanessa explained. "But a lot more simple to understand."

"So, you know where Leo is?" Mr. Schwimmer asked.

"I certainly do! And he's not far away at all!"

Where is Leo, the lost lifeguard?

K.I.D.S. Clues

Some maps use small pictures as symbols for special places on the map. To figure out what the pictures mean, you can look in the map key.

Map Key	
Picnic Area	
Office/Sign-In	
Rest Rooms	
Snack Bar	
Tennis Courts	

Name _____

A Lifeguard's Life

Here is the note that Leo wrote:

Hey, Schwim-man!

I'll be in the [☖] getting into my suit. Then I'm gonna grab a bite at the [☐] . I'll stop by the [✎] . If you're not there, I'm going to check out the [🎾] . Then I think I'll snatch a few z's at the [☂] .

Later, dude!

Leo

Now, solve the mystery! On a separate sheet of paper, rewrite Leo's note. Instead of the symbols, write in the words the symbols stand for.

Here is a map of the pool area.

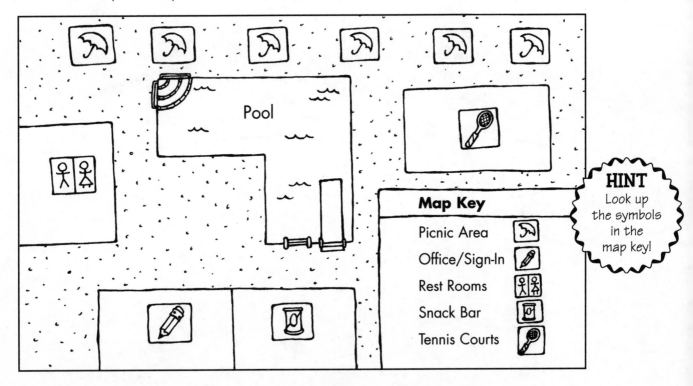

Map Key

Picnic Area

Office/Sign-In

Rest Rooms

Snack Bar

Tennis Courts

HINT
Look up the symbols in the map key!

Icky's Ice Cream

Maps can help us follow a route or path.

What a great day to be at the park! The sky was blue, the air was warm, and people were everywhere. Vanessa, Jasper, and Mari thought it was a great day to go in-line skating. They were just about to put on all their gear, when suddenly—

"Hey! That creep stole my ice cream cart!"

It was Mr. Icabod, the ice cream vendor. The kids all called him Icky for short.

"It looks like Icky's in some trouble," Mari observed.

"It also looks like a case for K.I.D.S.," said Vanessa. "Come on!"

By the time they reached Icky and the creep, a police officer was also there. Icky and the creep were arguing very loudly.

"I'm telling you, I didn't take it," said the creep. He was dressed in a spiffy suit and wore big, fancy shoes.

He had a smug smile on his face, and he looked like he didn't have a care in the world. The only thing out of place was the large spill of chocolate ice cream on his jacket.

"But you were the last person I served before I took my break. And you're still here now. You even have ice cream all over your suit," Icky said.

"So? I dropped my ice cream cone."

"Not with that much ice cream!" Icky shouted at the top of his lungs.

"Now, Mr. Icabod, calm down," Officer Miller said calmly. "I'm sure we can figure out what happened." She turned to the creep. "Why don't you tell us where you were while Mr. Icabod was on break?"

As the man spoke, Vanessa, Jasper, and Mari listened very closely. Jasper took notes. Vanessa dug a map of the park out of her pocket. And Mari watched a squirrel run up a tree.

Here is what the ice cream creep said:

"After I ordered a chocolate cone from this man here, I took a stroll through the park. I walked past the fountain, through the garden, and down to the lake. Then I followed the stream and crossed the bridge. I kept walking on this path. Eventually I found my way back here. I had walked a big circle around the park. When I got here, there was no ice cream cart, and no ice cream vendor. I assumed he had moved on."

Vanessa had a question for him. "Did you cross the bridge at the other end of the stream, or did you cross the same bridge you did before?"

"Uh, the other end, I guess," the creep said. "Like I said, the stroll I took was like a big circle around the park."

"I don't think so," Vanessa said.

The creep gulped. "You don't?"

"Nope. And not only are you lying, but I think I know where Icky's ice cream cart is."

How does Vanessa know the creep is lying? Where is Icky's ice cream cart?

K.I.D.S. Clues

Maps can help you follow the path someone took. Some symbols are pictures that can show land, water, landmarks, and help identify places along the way. 🌼 = Garden

Name _____

The Community Park

The paragraph below is the story told by the ice cream creep:

"After I ordered a chocolate cone from this man here, I took a stroll through the park. I walked past the fountain, through the garden, and down to the lake. Then I followed the stream and crossed the bridge. I kept walking on this path. Eventually I found my way back here. I had walked a big circle around the park."

Here is a map of the park. With a pencil, trace the route of the ice cream creep's walk, starting from where he bought the ice cream from Mr. Icabod.

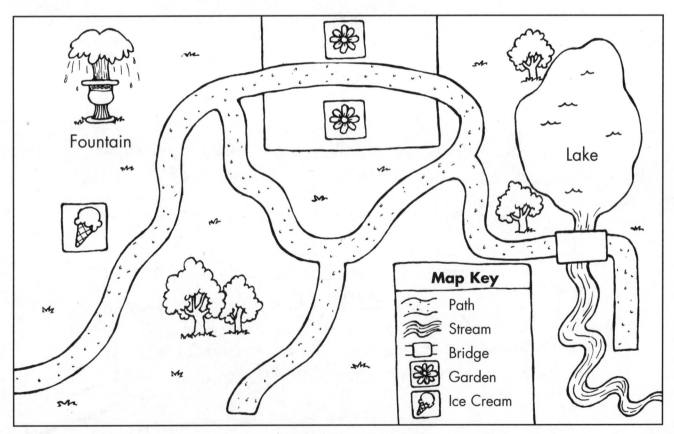

Fountain

Lake

Map Key
~ Path
≈ Stream
▭ Bridge
❀ Garden
🍦 Ice Cream

Where does the creep's story differ from the map? Circle this area.
This is where the missing ice cream cart is!

The Kidnapped Kitty

Floor plans sometimes use numbers instead of names to show where places and things are located.

Vanessa, Jasper, and Mari were at the mall with their parents. Their parents always seemed to go into shops that kids had no interest in, like all those clothing stores.

Jasper groaned at the unfairness of it all. "Parents should only take us to the mall when they shop for cool stuff."

"I agree," Vanessa said. "I could spend hours at the bookstore."

"Or the computer store," Jasper said.

"Or the pet store!" Mari added. "Speaking of which, do you think our parents would let us look at the puppies and kittens across the way?"

Vanessa and Jasper looked where Mari was pointing. The Pet Set pet shop was across from the Pants Palace.

It was better than waiting while their parents tried on clothes.

With their parents' permission to go to the pet store but nowhere else, Vanessa, Jasper, and Mari *ooh*-ed and *ah*-ed at the animals for sale.

"I know you should adopt animals from the pound, but these guys are so cute!" Mari said.

"Mr. Rumplemyer doesn't seem to think so," Jasper observed.

Mr. Rumplemyer, the pet store owner, was beside an empty cage, holding a note. He looked angry.

"What's wrong, Mr. Rumplemyer?" Vanessa asked.

"It's my son again," Mr. Rumplemyer said. "He's kidnapped one of our kitties."

Mari gasped. "Kidnapped a kitty?"

"Yes," Mr. Rumplemyer sighed. "He took the kitty. To get it back, I need to give him ten bags of dog biscuits for his dog, Rex. You see, I had told Ralph that he had to buy biscuits for his dog like everyone else. I can't just give him biscuits for free!" Mr. Rumplemyer sighed again. "So Ralph took a kitty and hid it somewhere, here at the mall."

"Did you give Ralph his biscuits?" Vanessa asked.

"Of course I did! The care of my pets is of utmost importance to me! Ralph took the biscuits, but instead of the kitty, he gave me this note."

Vanessa took the note and read it out loud. "Thanks, Pops, for the biscuits. Your kitty is safe and sound at the mall. To find her, follow these directions: Pants Palace, Book Gallery, Sports Central, CD Cellar, Cookie Nook."

"I called each store, but they didn't know what I was talking about," Mr. Rumplemyer sniffed. Mari sniffed along with him, thinking of the little lost kitty. "I don't know where to try next," he said.

"Don't worry, Mr. Rumplemyer," Vanessa said. "We'll help. We're K.I.D.S.!"

"I know you're kids," Mr. Rumplemyer began. "But—"

Jasper interrupted him. "No, K.I.D.S.—Keen-I Detective Services."

When Mr. Rumplemyer still didn't get it, Vanessa asked if he had a map of the mall. She, Jasper, and Mari placed the map on the counter. They marked each store from the note with the letter **X**.

Suddenly, Mari tapped the map. "I got it! I think I know where the kidnapped kitty is!"

Where did Ralph take the kidnapped kitty?

K.I.D.S. Clues

Names of shops in a mall are usually too long to fit in the small squares or rectangles on a floor plan. Instead, the stores are identified by numbers. To find the store, you can look it up in the map key, read the number, and then find that number on the floor plan.

Name _____

Mall Floor Plan

The map below shows the mall's floor plan. A number identifies each store. To find a store, look it up in the map key, then find the number on the map. Try it. Here are the stores from Ralph's list. Draw an **X** on the correct store on the map: Pants Palace, Book Gallery, Sports Central, CD Cellar, Cookie Nook.

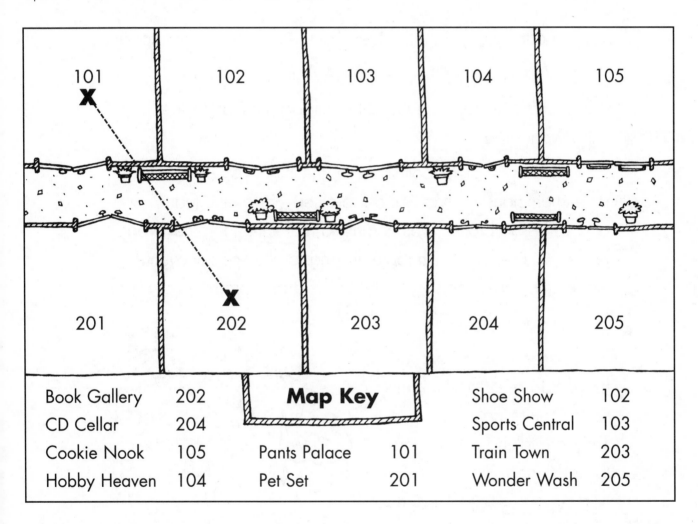

101	102	103	104	105
201	202	203	204	205

		Map Key		
Book Gallery	202		Shoe Show	102
CD Cellar	204		Sports Central	103
Cookie Nook	105	Pants Palace 101	Train Town	203
Hobby Heaven	104	Pet Set 201	Wonder Wash	205

Now draw lines to connect the **X**'s from left to right, crossing the mall as you go. The first line has been drawn for you.

What letter did you make? ____ The store names are listed alphabetically. Find the shop that begins with this letter. Write it here: _____

This is where the kidnapped kitty is. You solved the mystery!

Football Frenzy

Seating charts are maps that show where seats are inside a theater or stadium.

"I can't wait for the football game to start!" Jasper exclaimed.

"What's taking them so long?" Vanessa asked.

"Did you guys see the cute bulldog mascot on the field?" Mari wondered.

The high school football team, the Bulldogs, was in the state championship. Mari's older brother was on the team, and Vanessa's brother was hoping to make the team next year. Jasper just liked to watch football. And for the special event, the championship game was being held at a professional football stadium.

Jasper was so excited he could barely sit still in his seat. "You're right, Van. They *are* taking a long time to get started."

Vanessa pointed to the field. "I see the refs and coaches down there, talking in a big huddle.

I thought only the football players were supposed to huddle up."

"Something must be wrong," Jasper concluded. "Let's see what it is."

It wasn't easy getting down to the field. But when Mari told them who her brother was, the security guards let them through. Mari stopped to pet the team mascot, while Vanessa and Jasper walked to the edge of the huddle.

"Coach Fumble, what's the holdup?" Jasper asked.

The bothered coach ran a hand through his thinning hair. "Someone has stolen the footballs, son."

"Do you know who it is?" Vanessa asked, gaining new interest in the football game. This sounded like a mystery.

"We have a pretty good idea," Coach Fumble said. "We think it's Ryan Ruffhouse. He was cut from the team at the start of the season. He's been making our job hard all year."

"Why do you think it's Ryan?" Jasper asked, taking a pencil and paper from his jacket pocket.

"I found this note on the bulletin board in the locker room," Coach Fumble said, handing the note to Jasper.

Jasper read it and passed it to Vanessa. "It looks like a play-calling scheme," Jasper said.

"It is," Coach Fumble answered. "But it doesn't explain where the footballs are. And if we don't have footballs in ten minutes, there won't be a game."

"Don't worry, Coach," Vanessa said. "We'll find your footballs. After all, we're K.I.D.S.!"

"What can you kids do that we can't?"

"No, not *kids*," Jasper said, copying the note onto his paper. "K.I.D.S.—Keen-I—never mind."

Vanessa and Jasper walked up to Mari, who was still petting Buster, the bulldog. Just above Mari's head was a map of the stadium.

Jasper looked at the map, then looked at the paper in his hand. "That's it!" he shouted. "Let the games begin! I know where the footballs are!"

Where did Ryan Ruffhouse hide the footballs?

K.I.D.S. Clues

Most theaters and stadiums have a special kind of map called a seating chart. Seating charts show where sections of seats are. Because theaters and stadiums can be quite large, sections of seats are usually labeled with numbers. Each row of seats is labeled with a letter.

Name _____

Stadium Map

Look at this map of the stadium, upside down if it helps! Notice that each section has a number. The letters in each section are for the rows:

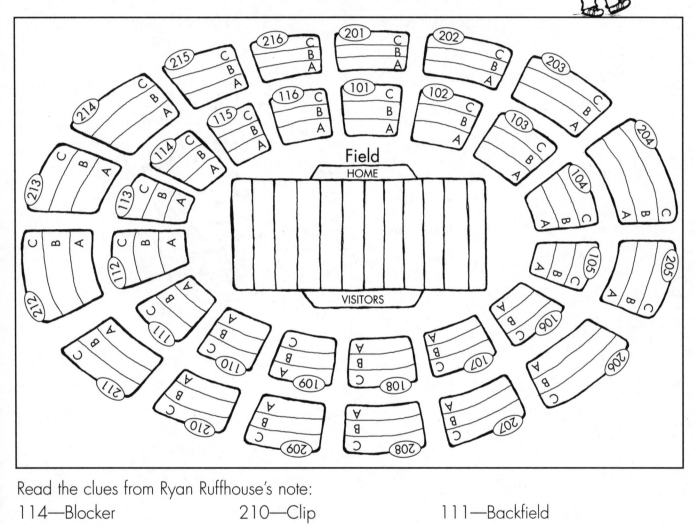

Read the clues from Ryan Ruffhouse's note:

114—Blocker   210—Clip   111—Backfield
216—Astro   208—Blitz   104—Call

Circle the first letter of each word. The first one has been done for you.

114—Ⓑlocker   _____   _____

_____   _____   _____

Now draw an **X** on each place Ryan has hidden a football. On the back of this page, explain how the clues helped you find the footballs.

The Mummy's Missing Jewel

Floor plans of public buildings (such as museums), often show places most visitors do not see.

"Take a look at this!" Vanessa exclaimed.

She was holding up the front page of the local newspaper. The headline read, "Museum Mummy Missing Jewel." The picture showed a close-up of a mummy, with a jewel on its chest.

The Daily Chronicle 50¢

MUSEUM MUMMY MISSING JEWEL

Jasper pointed to the mummy picture. "Cool! I didn't know the museum had mummies!"

"That's because you always pretend to be sick when we have field trips there," Mari reminded him. "I bet you don't know about all the live animal exhibits, either."

"Well, if I had known about the mummies, I probably would have gone."

Vanessa shook her head. "You guys are missing the point."

"What point?" Jasper asked, scratching his head.

"The missing jewel!" Vanessa told him. "It's the perfect mystery for K.I.D.S.!"

A half hour later, Vanessa, Jasper, and Mari stood in front of the case that held the mummy display. Yellow police tape was wrapped around the case, letting people know that something bad had happened. Along with the mummy, the large display case included lots of gold treasures and a few pieces of pottery. A painting of a pyramid hung on the back wall. The floor below the display case was covered with sand. At the other end of the room, a door stood ajar.

Vanessa peered at the museum brochure in her hand. "Here, guys. Take a look. This must be the missing jewel."

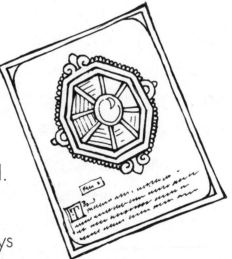

"Whoa!" Jasper exclaimed. "It looks like a ruby!"

"It is," Vanessa said. "It says here that the Ruby of Rhee-on was found with this mummy, lying over the mummy's heart, and held tightly with a small piece of the mummy's linen wrapping. The museum people unwrapped it and laid it on the mummy's chest so people could see it."

"So, everyone knew it was there," Jasper said.

"That means anyone could have taken it," Mari pointed out.

"Not necessarily," Vanessa said. "The door to each exhibit is locked securely every night."

"Look at those prints in the sand. They look like scratches," Mari said.

"I think they're our first clue," Vanessa said thoughtfully. She marked the scratches on the museum map in the brochure, drawing them exactly. Then she and Jasper started walking away from the mummy display, looking for more clues.

Mari was about to follow, when suddenly she stopped. Something about the scratches looked very familiar to her. "Wait!" she shouted.

Vanessa and Jasper came running back. "You know who stole the ruby?" Vanessa asked.

"Maybe. Let me see your map." Mari looked at the scratches Vanessa had drawn. She looked at the entire layout of the museum floor, including the areas they couldn't see behind the displays.

"I think I can solve the case!" said Mari. "I think I know who stole the mummy's jewel!"

Who stole the mummy's jewel?

K.I.D.S. Clues

When we look at something from ground level, or eye level, we don't always see the whole picture. Sometimes public buildings have hidden places that visitors don't have access to. By looking at a floor plan, you can see these places.

Name _____

Museum Map

Look at the map of the museum floor below. Find the mummy display. It has the scratches that Vanessa drew—the same scratches that she saw in the sand of the display case. Think about what the scratches look like. Who might have made them?

HINT Mari is an animal lover!

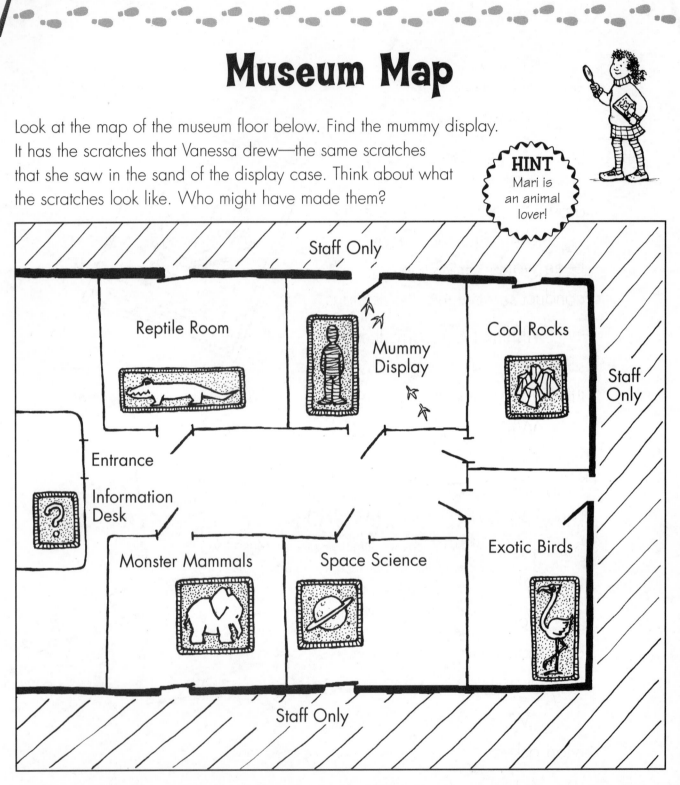

Follow the back halls, labeled "Staff Only," behind each display. Where do you think the jewel could be? Circle the display where Mari thinks the jewel is. Draw the jewel there, too.

On the back of this page, write a sentence that explains how you solved the mystery.

The Scatterbrained Scientist

*We can find things on maps by
using directions, such as left and right.*

The kids in Mr. Fuddleminder's science class had
been waiting all day. Mr. Fuddleminder was going to
conduct a very cool experiment. He'd told them that he'd
spent months finding the
right ingredients to make
the experiment a success.

What, exactly,
the experiment was
supposed to do, no one
knew. All they knew for
sure was that today was
the day!

Vanessa, Jasper,
and Mari were just as
excited as everyone else.

"What do you think his experiment will be about?"
Mari asked.

"I hope it's all bubbly and foamy!" Vanessa said.

"Or a big blast of fire!" Jasper added.

"Shh! Here comes Mr. Fuddleminder now," Mari said.

Mr. Fuddleminder looked like a cartoon character of the absentminded professor. He wore a long, white lab coat and his hair stuck up at crazy angles. And he was always twitching his hands.

Today, his hands were twitching more than normal.

"Well, class, I have some bad news," he announced. "I seem to have lost the ingredients for my special experiment. There will be no demonstration today."

The entire class let out a huge groan. No experiment meant listening and taking notes—not a fun way to spend science class.

Vanessa had other ideas. She raised her hand. "Mr. Fuddleminder, maybe we can help you find your ingredients."

"I don't see how that's possible, Vanessa, but thank you."

"Where did you last have them?" Vanessa continued.

"I had put them in my lab-coat pocket so I wouldn't lose

them," Mr. Fuddleminder explained. "Little did I realize that I had a hole in my pocket."

"Where else have you been?" Jasper asked, getting ready to jot down the details.

"Well, let's see," Mr. Fuddleminder began. "I walked down the hall, heading toward the gym, and turned right—no, left!—into

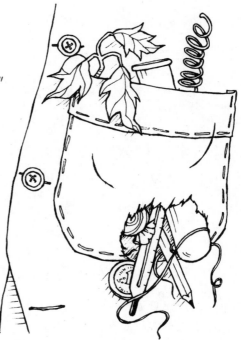

Mrs. Counter's room. I went back into the hall to walk toward the gym, when I took a left—no, a right!—turn into Mr. Harley's room. I was back in the hall, heading toward the gym again, when I went left—no, right!—into the storage closet. After that, I went back into the hallway to continue to the gym, when Mrs. Surenuff called me into her room. So I took a right—no, a left!—into her room. Finally, I went back into the hall and went right toward the gym."

"Did you look in the hall for the missing ingredients?" Mari asked.

"And the classrooms, too," Mr. Fuddleminder told her.

"I found some of the ingredients, but not all of them."

Vanessa had a sneaky suspicion that Mr. Fuddleminder had made a few mistakes. "I think I know what went wrong," she said. "I think we can help you find the magic ingredients!"

Where are Mr. Fuddleminder's lost ingredients?

K.I.D.S. Clues

Maps can be used to show you where to go. If you imagine yourself on the map and follow the directions, you can find yourself in a new place. Directions include such terms as *turn right*, *turn left*, and *keep going straight*.

Name _____

School Map

Look at the map below. It shows the hallway and the rooms. The labels inside each room tell you who the teacher is or the purpose of the room.

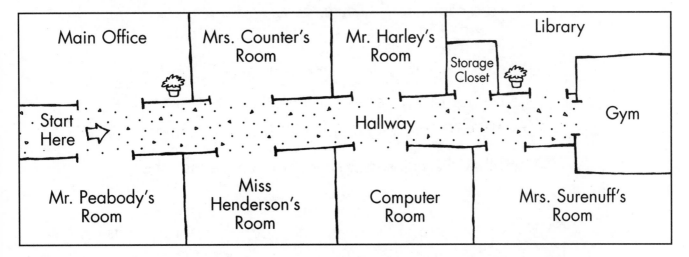

Read the paragraph below. Draw a star on the map in each room Mr. Fuddleminder mentions. Then circle the correct direction in the paragraph—right or left—to help Mr. Fuddleminder retrace his steps and find the lost ingredients for his experiment.

"I walked down the hall, heading toward the gym, and turned right—no, left!—into Mrs. Counter's room. I went back into the hall to walk toward the gym, when I took a left—no, a right!—turn into Mr. Harley's room. I was back in the hall, heading toward the gym again, when I went left—no, right!—into the storage closet. After that, I went back into the hallway to continue to the gym, when Mrs. Surenuff called me into her room. So I took a right—no, a left!—into her room. Finally, I went back into the hall and went right toward the gym."

Boris the Braggart

A map has a compass rose to show the directions north, south, east, and west.

For the past month, a family of ducks would waddle through the bushes during recess and wait patiently for kids to throw them pieces of bread. Mari fell in love with them instantly.

"Aren't they the cutest things you've ever seen?" she exclaimed.

Vanessa and Jasper liked animals, too—just not quite as much as Mari. And Jasper would much rather play kickball during recess, anyway.

"Sure, Mari," Vanessa said. "They're great."

"Look! The mother won't eat until all the ducklings get a piece first!" Mari observed.

Just then, Boris Dragbottom came slouching over. "You should see the ducks when no one else is around," Boris said. "They walk right up to you."

"How would you know?" Mari asked.

"Because I've been here early in the morning, all by myself. The big male duck took a piece of bread right from my fingers."

"I don't believe you!" Mari said.

Boris shrugged. "Suit yourself." And he walked away.

"Do you think he's telling the truth?" Mari asked Vanessa.

"All Boris ever does is brag," Vanessa reminded her. "I wouldn't believe anything Boris says."

Still, Mari couldn't forget it. So the next morning, with her mother along, she went to the school playground very early. She had a bag of old bread. She couldn't wait to see the ducks, and she hoped she could get one to eat out of her hand.

Mari and her mother waited and waited. They were still waiting when the first teacher pulled into the parking lot. They were still waiting when the first school bus arrived.

But no ducks.

Mari was more angry than disappointed. As soon as she saw Boris, she told him so. "You lied about the ducks, Boris, didn't you?"

"Nope," Boris said. "You just have to get here *really* early."

"And how early is that?"

"Well, I was on the swings when the sun came up over the slide," Boris said. "Were you here when the sun came up?"

"Um, no," Mari said, feeling silly for yelling at Boris. When she had a chance, she told Vanessa and Jasper what happened.

"I still don't believe him," Vanessa said. "And I think I know a way we can find out."

At recess that afternoon, Vanessa brought a compass from the classroom. She, Jasper, and Mari worked on drawing a map of the playground. The map included the directions *north*, *south*, *east*, and *west*. When they were finished, they had their answer.

"Boris was lying after all!" Vanessa said. "And we can prove it!"

How does Vanessa know that Boris is lying?

K.I.D.S. Clues

The needle on a compass always points north. When looking north on a compass, the direction opposite it is south, the direction to the right is east, and the direction to the left is west. Maps have a compass, too. It is called the compass rose. It shows where north, south, east, and west are. Another way to find directions is to remember that the sun always rises in the east and sets in the west.

Name _____

Playground Map

Here is the map that Vanessa, Jasper, and Mari drew of the playground. Circle the compass rose. It shows where north, south, east, and west are.

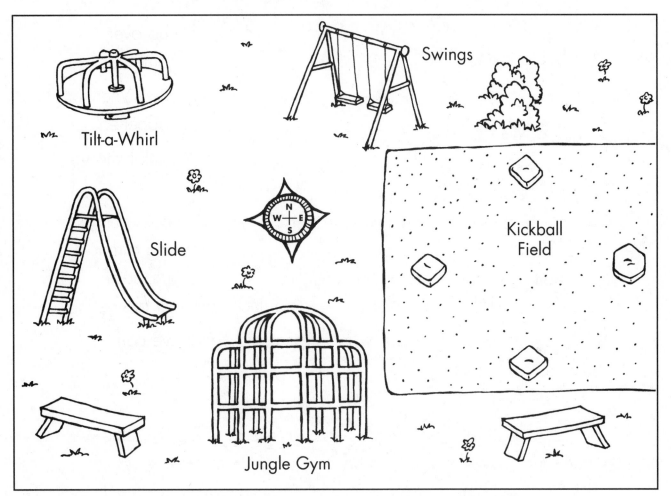

Follow these instructions to prove that Boris is lying:

1. Color in the slide. This is where Boris said the sun came up.

2. Look at the compass rose. Find the east side of the playground.
   This is where the sun will rise. Draw a yellow sun here.

How do you know Boris is lying? Write your idea on the lines below.

_____

_____

_____

The Mysterious Monsters

The cardinal directions north, south, east, and west help us find places on a map. Maps can also show details such as landmarks.

"Monsters, I tell you!" Mr. Saggerate said to Mrs. Bluebell one afternoon.

"Oh, nonsense!" Mrs. Bluebell said in return. "Our town does not have monsters."

"Well, I saw them!" Mr. Saggerate waved his arms dramatically—so dramatically that he caught the attention of Vanessa, Jasper, and Mari.

"What's the problem, Mr. Saggerate?" Vanessa asked.

"It's too terrible to tell you nice children!" Mr. Saggerate said worriedly.

Mrs. Bluebell shook her head. "Mr. Saggerate thinks he's seeing monsters at night, on his way home from work."

"Monsters!" Jasper said with a gleam in his eye. "Cool!"

Mr. Saggerate owned a bookstore in town. Mrs. Bluebell owned the flower shop next door. Everyone knew that Mr. Saggerate got so excited about his reading that he would start to think fictional stories were real. There was a time when he thought aliens were taking over the town.

"What are you reading these days?" Mrs. Bluebell asked.

"Um . . . *Monsters From Below*," admitted Mr. Saggerate.

"I guess this mystery's solved," Jasper said, disappointed.

"Maybe not," Vanessa said thoughtfully. "Where, exactly, did you see these monsters, Mr. Saggerate?"

"I don't want you kids involved," Mr. Saggerate said.

"That's okay," Mari told him. "We're K.I.D.S.!"

"We know that, dear," Mrs. Bluebell said. "That's why—"

"No, K-I-D-S," Jasper spelled.

"Yes, that's how you spell *kids*," Mr. Saggerate agreed.

"No. We're—oh, never mind," Vanessa said. "So, where *did* you see the monsters?" Jasper took out a pen and paper and wrote down what Mr. Saggerate said. Here it is:

"I came out of my shop around 9:00 P.M. The sun was down, so it was pretty dark. I headed east on Main Street, then turned north on Fountain Avenue. When I came to the intersection of Fountain and Elm, I saw the first monster! I quickly went east on Elm until I came to Maple Drive. Then I walked south. Where Maple crosses Broadway, I saw another monster! So, I ran east on Broadway and headed south at River Road. At Highland Avenue, I turned west.

As I headed north into my driveway, I saw another monster! I ran inside and closed the door. By morning, the monsters were gone!"

"Mr. Saggerate, do you have a map of the town?" Vanessa asked.

"Why, yes. Just a minute." Mr. Saggerate disappeared inside his bookstore, then came back out with a map. Vanessa, Jasper, and Mari spread the map out on the sidewalk, then compared it with Mr. Saggerate's walk home.

"You didn't see any monsters, Mr. Saggerate! And we can prove it!" Jasper said, excitedly.

What did Mr. Saggerate see, if they weren't monsters?

K.I.D.S. Clues

Some maps include details about a place, such as landmarks and important buildings. They may be labeled, or sometimes you might find what they represent in the map key. If you're using a map to find a landmark or important building, use the compass rose. It shows the four main directions on a map (north, south, east, and west).

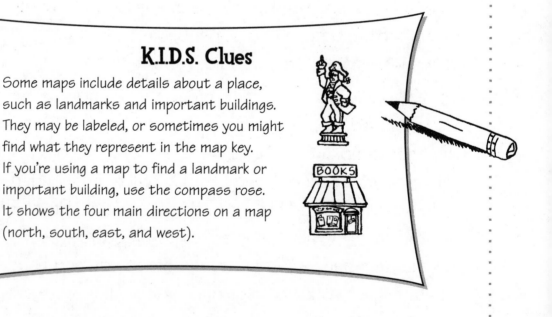

Name _____

Monster Sightings

Read Mr. Saggerate's story below. As you do, trace a path on the town map (page 58) to show Mr. Saggerate's route. First, find the bookstore. Draw an **X** here. Then, as you follow his path home, circle each area where Mr. Saggerate saw a monster.

"I came out of my shop around 9:00 P.M. The sun was down, so it was pretty dark. I headed east on Main Street, then turned north on Fountain Avenue. When I came to the intersection of Fountain and Elm, I saw the first monster! I quickly went east on Elm until I came to Maple Drive. Then I walked south. Where Maple crosses Broadway, I saw another monster! So, I ran east on Broadway and headed south at River Road. At Highland Avenue, I turned west. As I headed north into my driveway, I saw another monster! I ran inside and closed the door. By morning, the monsters were gone!"

Now write what the monsters really were.

1. _____

2. _____

3. _____

Name _____

Town Map

Here is a map of the town. Follow the route Mr. Saggerate took from his store (page 57).
Circle the objects that might have been the monsters Mr. Saggerate thought he saw.

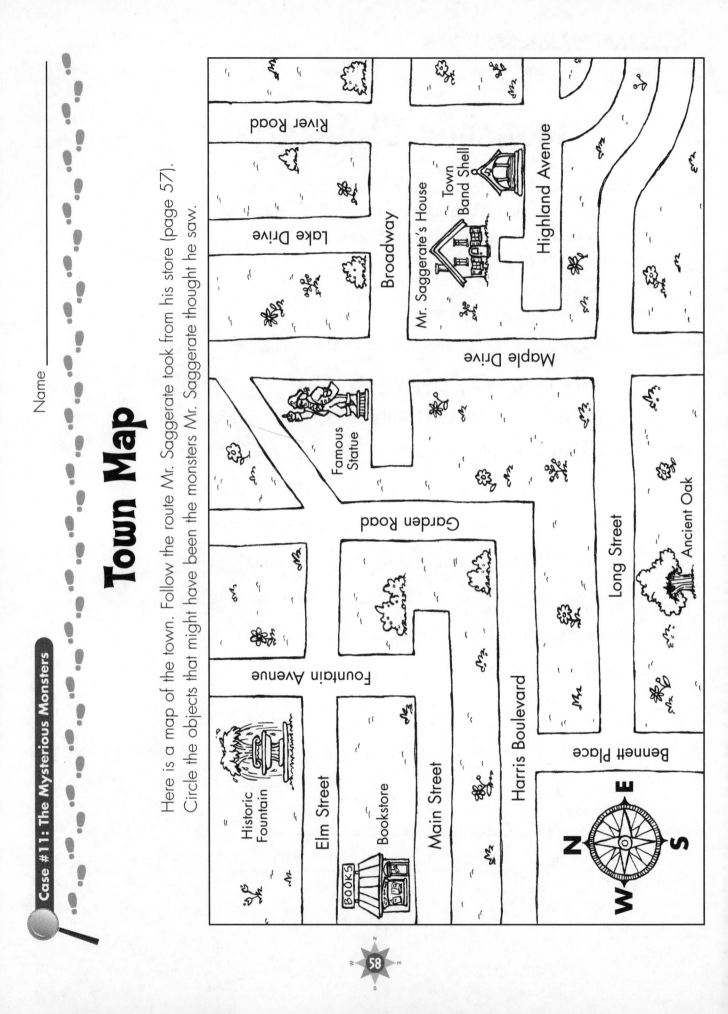

The Missing Millionaire

Sometimes a compass rose will show intermediate directions (northeast, southeast, southwest, and northwest). Using those directions can help us find things between north, south, east, and west on a map. A map scale shows how the size of places on a map compare to the real size of places on earth.

Mayor Worriwort had a mystery that needed to be solved. In fact, he'd placed an ad in the local paper, asking people to help solve the mystery.

"Take a look at this!" Vanessa said, once she and the rest of the detectives of K.I.D.S. were settled at the club-house. ("The rest" were, of course, Jasper and Mari.)

"*Mayor Miffed Over Missing Millionaire*," Jasper read.

"Missing millionaire?" Mari repeated. "I didn't know our town had any millionaires!"

"It doesn't," Vanessa confirmed. "However, a very famous millionaire was trying to travel around the world in a hot-air balloon."

"Oh! I read about that!" Jasper jumped in. "He had

this gigantic balloon that took off from, like, Australia, or something."

"That's right," Vanessa nodded. "He was supposed to pass by our town a few days ago, but he seems to have just disappeared. No one can find him."

"Did the balloon crash?" Mari asked.

"They don't think so. The millionaire didn't alert anyone that he was in trouble."

"That doesn't make any sense, then," Jasper said. "How could a millionaire and a huge hot-air balloon just disappear?"

"There's the mystery!" Vanessa announced. "Let's see if we can figure it out. First, we'll need a map."

As Mari went off in search of a map, Vanessa read off the millionaire balloonist's last sightings. Jasper wrote them down in an orderly list, recording the distance and the direction.

"I bet the millionaire's adventures would make an excellent adventure comic book!" Jasper said.

When Mari returned, they spread the map out over

the floor of the clubhouse. Jasper read off the directions and distances. Using a ruler, Vanessa and Mari worked to pinpoint exactly where the millionaire and his balloon were last seen.

"That can't be!" Mari said. "It looks like the millionaire just disappeared into Molehill Mountain."

"And if he crashed, they would have found his hot-air balloon," Jasper added.

"Maybe not," Vanessa said. She, Jasper, and Mari studied the map some more, deep in thought.

Suddenly, Jasper snapped his fingers. "I got it!" he shouted. "I think I know where the missing millionaire is!"

Where is the missing millionaire and his hot-air balloon?

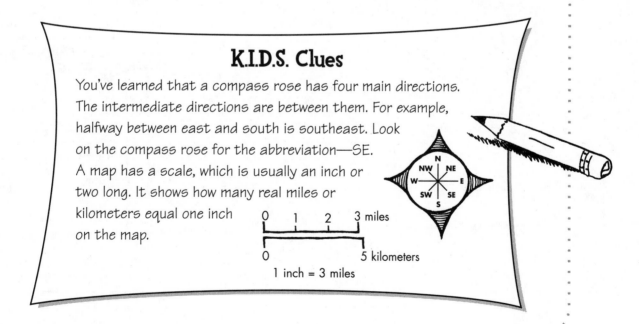

K.I.D.S. Clues

You've learned that a compass rose has four main directions. The intermediate directions are between them. For example, halfway between east and south is southeast. Look on the compass rose for the abbreviation—SE. A map has a scale, which is usually an inch or two long. It shows how many real miles or kilometers equal one inch on the map.

0   1   2   3 miles

0   5 kilometers

1 inch = 3 miles

The Flight of the Missing Millionaire

Here is the flight of the missing millionaire:

1) 9 miles southeast   **2)** 3 miles east   **3)** 9 miles northeast

Here is a map of the area he flew over. Find the scale on the map, then get a ruler. Measure the scale. You'll see that it is one inch. One inch on this map equals three real miles. Follow the directions, starting from the top of the hot-air balloon, and mark the balloon's flight with **X**'s. Circle the place where the balloon was last seen. The first part of the millionaire's flight has been marked for you.

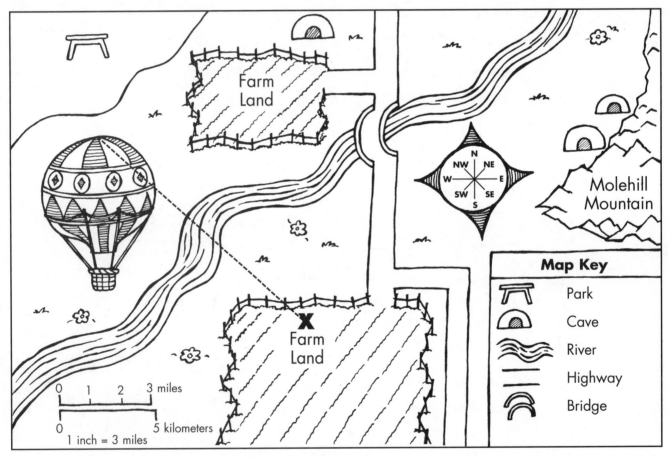

What symbol do you see near your circle? Draw it here: _____

Look up the symbol in the map key. What does it stand for? _____

Where might the missing millionaire be? Write your ideas on the back of this page. Be sure to explain what he did with his hot-air balloon.

Boris the Braggart Strikes Again

Maps can show natural and man-made borders.

"My family spent summer vacation at Lake Lulu!" Mari told her school friends outside at recess.

Vanessa and Jasper had already heard all about it. They'd already heard how Mari and her family had saved a lost baby deer and helped it find its mother. They'd already heard how Mari had watched a family of baby turtles hatch from their eggs beside the lake and take their first swim.

"And then we helped a park ranger relocate a family of beavers who were building a den too close to a neighborhood!" Mari said.

"Oh, yeah? That's nothing," Boris Dragbottom said as he sauntered up. "My family and I herded a whole head of cattle out West."

"You did not!" Mari said.

"Did too," Boris replied. "Being a cowboy beats staying at Lake Lulu any old summer."

Vanessa and Jasper looked at each other. Boris Dragbottom not only had a bad habit of exaggerating and bragging, he often lied to make his stories sound more exciting. And this sounded like one of Boris's best stories ever.

"Sounds like fun, Boris," Jasper said slowly.

"Sure does," Vanessa agreed, nodding her head. "I bet you saw lots of different states out West."

Boris cocked his head and smiled. A few other kids had gathered around. He was attracting quite an audience. Everyone wanted to hear about his cowboy adventures.

"We went through a lot of them," Boris said, now chewing on a piece of grass.

"I'd love to hear about it," Jasper said, knowing what Vanessa was up to. "It sounds like it would make a great adventure comic book." He took out a sheet of paper and a pencil, ready to take notes.

Boris shifted his feet, preparing to tell his story. "First," he said importantly, "we met with the cowboys in Montana. They told us that we had to take the cows all the way to Texas. That's over a thousand miles."

A bunch of kids who had gathered around *ooh*-ed and *ah*-ed.

"After they made sure we could ride a horse pretty well, we were off. We drove the cattle—not in a car, of course; *drove* is a special cowboy word—from Montana to Wyoming. Then we went south into Colorado. From Colorado we went south to Idaho, then into New Mexico, where we crossed the Missouri River. Finally we got into Texas. We followed the Rocky Mountains south the whole time."

"Wow!" Mari exclaimed, not realizing that Boris was telling a tall tale. "That sounds exciting!"

"It was better than your trip to Lake Lulu," Boris bragged.

"It would be—if it had really happened," Vanessa declared.

"Of course it happened!" Boris yelled.

"No it didn't, Boris," Jasper said. "And we can prove it once we get back to class."

How do Jasper and Vanessa know that Boris is telling a tall tale?

K.I.D.S. Clues

Countries have borders, as do towns, counties, and states. Borders are imaginary lines made by people to show where one place ends and another begins. When borders haven't been created by natural landforms like rivers or lakes, map makers show borders with lines.

Boris's Cattle Drive

This is the map Boris' family used on their trip. Lines show the borders between the states. Mountains, rivers, and lakes are drawn in. The map key tells what each symbol means.

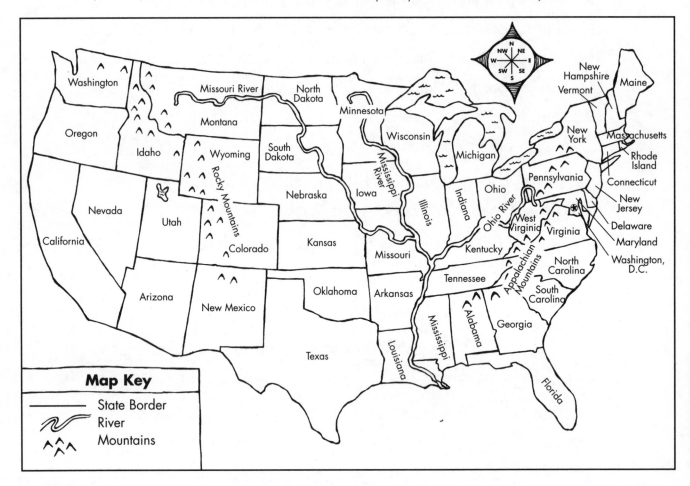

Here are the states, in order, that Boris said he went to on his cattle drive: Montana, Wyoming, Colorado, Idaho, New Mexico, and Texas.

• Find each state and put a star in it.

• Then connect the stars—in Boris's order.

• Find the Missouri River. Color it blue.

• Find the Rocky Mountains. Color them brown.

On the back of this page, explain how finding the states, the river, and the mountains prove that Boris was lying about his summer vacation.

Railroad Rudy

Maps can show train routes.

"How many days has it been now?" Mari asked Jasper, who was reading the paper at the clubhouse.

"Hmm. Let's see. It says here that a local college student named Rudy Reckleman left by train six days ago. He was only supposed to be gone for a weekend."

"Six days!" Mari exclaimed. "His mother must be a wreck!"

"She is a wreck," Vanessa announced, coming through the clubhouse door. "She's just hired the services of K.I.D.S.!"

"Really?" Jasper said. Jumping up, he grabbed his notebook and a pen. It sounded like Rudy was on a railroad adventure. And a great adventure made a great action-adventure comic book.

"What did Mrs. Reckleman say?" Mari asked.

"She wants us to meet with her at her home," Vanessa informed them.

Mari scratched her head. "But aren't the police helping her? What can we do that they can't?"

Vanessa and Jasper sighed.

"We're detectives," Vanessa said. "We might see something the police haven't."

"I guess you're right," Mari agreed. "Let's go!"

A half hour later they were seated around Mrs. Reckleman's kitchen table, eating oatmeal cookies and drinking lemonade.

"In the paper, the police said that Rudy's been sending you postcards," Vanessa said.

"That's right. I've been getting one postcard a day. Oh, dear! If only I knew where he was going next! I could meet him and talk to him about coming home!"

"May we see the postcards, Mrs. Reckleman?" Mari asked.

"Certainly, dear." Mrs. Reckleman shuffled out of the kitchen, then came back in with a stack of postcards.

"They're in order, from first to last."

"Do you have a map, Mrs. Reckleman?" Vanessa asked. "I think we'd have a better chance of finding Rudy if we could see each of these places on a map."

Mrs. Reckleman shuffled off again, while the detectives of K.I.D.S. finished the oatmeal cookies. When she returned, they unfolded the map and spread it across the table. Working with Mrs. Reckleman, they found each town and circled it with a big red marker. When they finished, they sat back and looked at it.

"Well?" Mrs. Reckleman asked. "Can you figure out where my son is going next?"

"I think we can!" Vanessa said.

Where will Rudy Reckleman go next?

K.I.D.S. Clues

Some maps have symbols for train tracks. They show the paths of actual train routes. The map key shows the symbol for the train tracks, and sometimes even the train stations.

69

Name _____

Tracking Down Railroad Rudy

The postcards below show the towns where Rudy has been:

Find each of these towns on the map below. Circle them.

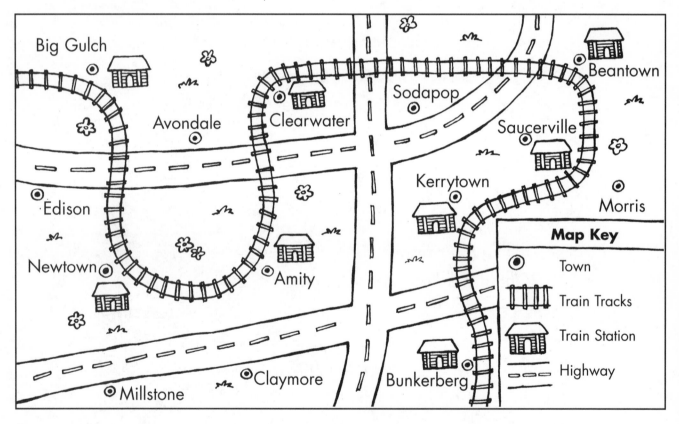

What is the symbol for a town? Draw it here. _____

What is the symbol for a train station? Draw it here. _____

Which two towns might Rudy go to next? _____

How do you know? _____

_____

70

The Scary Scavenger Hunt

Maps can have lines that run across and down, forming a grid. The grid is labeled with numbers and letters. The grid helps pinpoint a location (place) on the map.

Every fall, Mrs. Winkleheffer opened her house to all the kids in the neighborhood for a scavenger hunt. Mrs. Winkleheffer was a nice older lady whose children had all grown up and moved away. Mr. Winkleheffer liked to watch sports on TV. They lived in a very old house at the edge of town. Some kids thought the house was haunted. But the only things that "haunted" Mrs. Winkleheffer's home were a dozen or so cats. Mrs. Winkleheffer could never turn away a stray.

Mari thought Mrs. Winkleheffer was the best.

For the rest of the kids, the fall scavenger hunt was the best. They pretended they were creeping around a real haunted house, looking for cool, and sometimes scary, things.

And this year, the list of hidden treasures for the scavenger hunt seemed especially mysterious and exotic.

"A rubber black widow spider!" Jasper exclaimed, looking at the list.

"Eyeball of newt!" Vanessa read.

"The Orb of Orzibon!" Mari said. "What do you think that is?"

"We won't know until we find it!" Vanessa pointed out. So, with about 20 other kids, Vanessa, Jasper, and Mari began searching through Mrs. Winkleheffer's backyard, the scavenger hunt having officially begun.

However, after a full hour of searching, nobody had found anything. Not even the detective skills of K.I.D.S. were of any help.

Mrs. Winkleheffer appeared on her back porch. "No luck, kids?" she clapped, a gleam in her eye.

"You've outdone yourself this year," Mari said. "We can't find anything! Are you sure you've hidden stuff for us to find?"

"Of course, sugar! Perhaps you just need a few clues." Mrs. Winkleheffer disappeared back inside.

At the word *clues*, Vanessa perked up. Clues meant only one thing to her—mystery!

When Mrs. Winkleheffer returned, she carried a stack of papers. Walking off the porch, she handed them out. "This is a map of the backyard," she said. "The map will help you find the items on this year's scavenger hunt. And don't forget—the winner gets a kitten from a new litter, born just a few weeks ago!"

Mari was excited. "We *have* to win the scavenger hunt now! Let me see that map."

Vanessa and Jasper crowded around. On the map were listed the items from the scavenger hunt, with letters and numbers written beside them.

"These letters and numbers must be for the grid on the map!" Mari whispered so the other kids wouldn't hear her.

"You're right!" Vanessa said.

"I don't think anyone else has figured it out," Jasper

said, pointing to the rest of the kids crowded around their maps. "Let's see if we can quietly find everything on the list!"

Where has Mrs. Winkleheffer hidden things in her backyard?

K.I.D.S. Clues

A grid helps pinpoint a location (place) on a map. To find a location on a grid map, you trace one finger across the letter column. Then you trace another finger down the number row. When your fingers meet (or the column and row intersect), the correct location has been found. These letters and numbers can also be called *coordinates*.

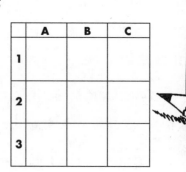

	A	B	C
1			
2			
3			

Name _____

Mrs. Winkleheffer's Scavenger Hunt

Look at this map of Mrs. Winkleheffer's backyard. Pay special attention to the boxes on the grid map. Notice that they are labeled with letters across the top and numbers down the side.

Here are the items for the scavenger hunt, along with their coordinates. Circle each place on the map. On the lines below, write where each item for the scavenger hunt was found.

rubber spider	D3	_____
Orb of Orzibon	C2	_____
eyeball of newt	A1	_____
pearl of wisdom	D4	_____
stuffed horned toad	B3	_____
ring of bat feathers	A4	_____

Super Sleuth Solutions

Case #1 The Hiding Hamster

When Vanessa compared her map to Carmen's map, she noticed that something was missing—the box on Carmen's bedside table. Vanessa concluded that the box must have fallen off the table when Carmen was cleaning. Since Harry and the box were both missing, Vanessa figured they were together. When they moved the bedside table, they found the box underneath—with Harry cozily sleeping inside. Case closed by K.I.D.S.!

Case #2 Mrs. Readsalot's Brooch

Vanessa figured that Mrs. Readsalot's brooch would be in the one area she had visited most. However, Mrs. Readsalot had spent about the same amount of time in each room of the library. Vanessa drew lines on the map to show where Mrs. Readsalot had walked. When she did, she noticed the one place Mrs. Readsalot had passed most—the big plant in the middle of the library! When Mrs. Readsalot searched the plant, her brooch was there. It had been hard to see before because it looked like a butterfly. Another success story for Vanessa and K.I.D.S.!

Case #3 The Silly Surf Dude

When Vanessa saw the map of the beach, she realized that only one path came out of the dunes. And it was right next to the rest rooms, not the snack bar. Since Chip said he didn't pass any other buildings, Vanessa suggested that maybe he had stopped at the rest rooms before the snack bar. When Chip thought about it, he smacked his head, called himself a silly dude, and realized that he had stopped there first. When they went to the rest-room area, Chip's surfboard was leaning up against the wall of the building, just where he'd left it. What once was lost was found!

Case #4 The Lost Lifeguard

When Vanessa compared the pictures in Leo's letter with the symbols on the map of the pool area, she discovered that they were the same! Reading Leo's note was like filling in the words of a secret code. First, Leo was going to change into his suit at the rest rooms. Then he was going to get something to eat at the snack bar. Afterward, he would meet Mr. Schwimmer at the office/sign-in desk. If Mr. Schwimmer wasn't there, Leo was going to the tennis courts. Then he would take a nap in the picnic area. This is where they found Leo. The kids at the pool could finally swim again, and K.I.D.S. had solved another case!

Case #5 Icky's Ice Cream

As the ice cream creep told his story, Vanessa followed his route on her map of the park. When he said his walk had been like a circle, Vanessa saw that he would have had to cross the stream a second time, since he'd crossed it once. But from the creep's story, that's not possible. Only one bridge crosses the stream, and the path on the other side leads to a dead end. Vanessa figured that the creep had taken the cart over the bridge and hidden it there, because it was here that his story didn't make sense. Officer Miller, the detectives of K.I.D.S., Icky, and the creep took their own stroll and found the missing ice cream cart. Score another one for K.I.D.S.!

Case #6 The Kidnapped Kitty

As Mari studied the **X**'s they'd drawn on the mall map, she noticed that they made a zigzag pattern (101, 202, 103, 204, 105). By connecting the **X**'s, she made a large letter **W**. Wonder Wash laundromat was the only store that started with **W**. Mari thought about her own cat. She remembered how it loved to sleep in laundry baskets, with clean clothes warm from the dryer. Mari quickly told Mr. Rumplemyer to call Wonder Wash. When he did, the kidnapped kitty was found, safe and sound.

Case #7 Football Frenzy

When Jasper saw the map of the stadium, he realized that some of the section numbers on the map were the same as the numbers on Ryan's note. He suspected that the first letter of each word might be for the rows. He, Vanessa, and Mari spread out, each taking a couple of sections. The footballs were found in each numbered section in the lettered rows (114-B, 216-A, 210-C, 208-B, 111-B, 104-C). They returned the footballs to Coach Fumble, and the Bulldogs won the state championship.

Case #8 The Mummy's Missing Jewel

Mari recognized the scratches in the sand, but she wasn't sure how such scratches could get onto the floor of the mummy exhibit. When she looked at the museum map, she found her answer. Although museum visitors were not aware of it, hallways behind the displays connected each display. Every night the doors to the exhibits were locked tight, but Mari had noticed the staff-only door at the back of the mummy display was left ajar. Mari followed the hallways until she found what she was looking for—an exhibit of exotic birds. She had recognized the scratches as similar to the footprints her green Amazon parrot, Bubba, made at home. When the detectives of K.I.D.S. went to the bird exhibit, they saw the missing jewel in a parrot's cage. The jewel was retrieved, and K.I.D.S. had another success story!

Case #9 · The Scatterbrained Scientist

As Mr. Fuddleminder told his story, Vanessa observed that he was confused as to which way he went. She drew a map of the hallway and rooms going off it and labeled each room accordingly. Then she had Jasper read back the rooms Mr. Fuddleminder said he'd been into (left into Mrs. Counter's room, left into Mr. Harley's room, left into the storage closet, right into Mrs. Surenuff's room, and right into the gym). Following their own map and directions, they searched the correct classrooms for Mr. Fuddleminder's lost ingredients. All the ingredients were found, and the experiment went off without a hitch.

Case #10 · Boris the Braggart

Vanessa, Jasper, and Mari first made a map of the playground, drawing in the playground equipment. Using the compass, they figured out where north was, then they drew a compass rose on the map. Boris said when he sat on the swings the sun rose over the slide, but the slide is to the west of the swings. The sun would have risen over the kickball field. Since Boris incorrectly described where the sun rose, Vanessa, Jasper, and Mari concluded that Boris the Braggart was once again bragging about something he didn't do. He was the unlucky duck this time! Case closed!

Case #11 · The Mysterious Monsters

Using the directions and street names Mr. Saggerate described, Vanessa, Jasper, and Mari followed his route on the map. They circled each place where he saw a monster. And each place had a small picture and label of a town landmark. Vanessa convinced Mr. Saggerate that instead of monsters, he had seen the same landmarks he'd walked by every evening (the Historic Fountain, the Famous Statue, and the Town Band Shell). The dark—and his imagination—had turned them into monsters.

Case #12 · The Missing Millionaire

When Jasper, Mari, and Vanessa used the map scale and compass rose to figure out the flight of the hot-air balloon, they ended up at Molehill Mountain. At the base of Molehill Mountain, Jasper saw this symbol, , which told him that the mountain had caves. Thinking like an eccentric millionaire, Jasper concluded that the adventurer had landed at the base of the mountain and deflated his balloon. He'd then stored it in one of the caves. When K.I.D.S. called the mayor's office and told the mayor their idea, he sent out a team of rescuers, who found the missing millionaire. It turns out that the millionaire decided he was bored with the hot-air balloon, and he was *spelunking*, or cave exploring, and camping in one of the caves. He was safe and unharmed, and K.I.D.S. were heroes for a day.

Case #13 Boris the Braggart Strikes Again

As soon as recess was over and everyone was back in class, Jasper and Vanessa asked if they could pull down the classroom wall map of the United States. They then repeated the states, in the same order Boris had listed them when he described his vacation. Using the map, they pointed out that it was impossible, not to mention silly, to travel from Colorado to Idaho and then to New Mexico. In addition, Boris couldn't have crossed the Missouri River in New Mexico because the river does not go through New Mexico. One more mistake—Boris said his family followed the Rocky Mountains south the whole time, but they would not have been going south if they traveled from Colorado toward Idaho. Boris's story made no sense. When faced with these facts, Boris admitted that although he had spent the summer with horses and cows, it wasn't out West—it was at Lake Lulu. Boris the Braggart was found out again!

Case #14 Railroad Rudy

As Vanessa studied the towns they'd circled on the map, she realized that each town was along a train route. And, each town that Rudy had sent a postcard from had a train station. If Rudy continued on the same train, the next postcard they'd get would be from Kerrytown. When Mrs. Reckleman got the postcard from Kerrytown, she told the police the theory that K.I.D.S. had come up with. The next town on the train route was Bunkerberg. Mrs. Reckleman felt better knowing where Rudy was headed, and she was able to call him at the Bunkerberg train station.

Case #15 The Scary Scavenger Hunt

Vanessa, Mari, and Jasper first circled each correct grid-map box, according to the coordinates provided by Mrs. Winkleheffer. They then searched each circled area (the birdbath, the rosebush, the flowerpot, the birdhouse, the doghouse, and the chair). When they did so, they found all the items for the scavenger hunt. Mari (with permission from her parents) brought home a new kitten, and K.I.D.S. had another success story.

Notes